Puppy
Care

A Guide to Loving and Nurturing Your Pet

Puppy
Care

A GUIDE TO LOVING AND
NURTURING YOUR PET

KIM DENNIS-BRYAN

LONDON, NEW YORK, MUNICH, MELBOURNE, AND DELHI

WRITTEN AND EDITED BY Kim Dennis-Bryan FZS
CONSULTANTS Julius Neuman BVSc (Hons), MRCVS;
Menas Beaca DVM, MRCVS, & Lisa Guiney VN,
of The Mayhew Animal Home and Humane
Education Centre, London, UK
ORIGINAL SERIES STYLING Lisa Lanzarini
DESIGNERS Cathy Tincknell and Lynne Moulding
DTP DESIGNER Dean Scholey
PUBLISHING MANAGER Cynthia O'Neill Collins
ART DIRECTOR Mark Richards
CATEGORY PUBLISHER Alex Kirkham
PRODUCTION Claire Pearson

First American Edition, 2004

Published in the United States by
DK Publishing, Inc.
375 Hudson Street
New York, New York 10014

04 05 06 07 08 10 9 8 7 6 5 4 3 2

The publisher would like to thank the following for their kind
permission to reproduce their photographs:

(Key: a-above; c-center; b-below; l-left; r-right; t-top)

Ardea London Ltd: John Daniels 21tr. Christopher Bryan 45tl.
RSPCA: Angela Hampton 33tr, 33cr.

All other images © Dorling Kindersley Picture Library:
Andy Crawford: 15, 18cra, 22cl, 23bcr, 27tr, 27tl, 27cla, 27cl. Steve
Lyne: 4-5, 6bl, 7, 8bl, 12cr, 13, 14bl, 16-17c, 18bl, 18-19c, 19br,
19tc, 20c, 20bl, 20clb, 20-21c, 22cr, 22-23c, 24bl, 24c, 25, 27b, 27cl,
27cla, 27tl, 28c, 28bl, 28-29, 29cra, 30tl, 31, 32tl, 32-33, 34b, 35,
36-37, 38l, 38bc, 38br, 38cr, 39, 40-41b, 41, 42bl, 43, 45l, 47bl.

A Cataloging-in-Publication record
for this book is available from
the Library of Congress.

ISBN 0-7566-0910-0

Reproduced by Colourscan, Singapore
Printed and bound in Italy by L.E.G.O.

Discover more at
www.dk.com

NOTE TO PARENTS This book teaches children how to be caring, responsible dog owners. However, your child will need help and support from you, or a professional, in all aspects of their puppy's care. Don't let your child have a puppy unless you are certain that your family has the time and resources to look after it for its entire life. When you see the sign "!" in a blue circle, you should take special note.

NOTE TO CHILDREN In this book we say *either* "he" *or* "she" when we talk about how to look after your puppy. This changes depending on whether the puppy in the photo is a boy or a girl, but the advice we give applies to puppies of both sexes.

Contents

Introduction

EVERYONE LOVES PUPPIES. These little animals are friendly and playful, and enjoy life to the fullest, from the moment they wake until they fall asleep again. Puppies depend on us for a proper education and exercise as well as affection, food, and a comfortable bed. Your actions and decisions will determine how your puppy grows up. Training him to be well-behaved and obedient is fun, but takes time.

Your dog will be your best friend all his life. Make sure you care for him well.

Think carefully

Having a pet requires commitment from the whole family. You must decide if you have time to bond with, exercise, groom, and train a puppy. Dogs vary a lot in size, so think about the space you have for a dog, too. Having a puppy is not a short-term commitment. A healthy dog lives 12 years or more, so you should think about the costs involved in keeping a dog over a long period.

All dogs need daily exercise. Do you have time to walk your dog every day?

WHICH TYPE OF DOG?

- Do you want a large or small breed? (See pp.8–9 and p.46.)
- Do you want a short-, wire-, or long-haired dog? (See pp.26–27 and p.46.)
- Do you want a purebred or mixed-breed dog? (See pp.8–9 and p46.)

Behavioral traits

All puppies have their own unique
personalities, but purebred
puppies behave in a more
predictable way. Some
purebreds are calmer, more
friendly, and easier to train
than other kinds. These
qualities are more
important than what
a puppy looks like.

*Most Labrador retriever
puppies make good family
pets, growing up to be loyal,
gentle, and eager to please.*

*Puppies with laid-
back personalities
settle in to a new
home quickly and
will enjoy meeting
your friends.*

Family dogs

Dogs that are going to be part of a
family should not be too large, too
energetic, or too protective. They
should be gentle and learn
quickly how to behave. These
traits are seen in many herding
and sporting dogs. They make
very popular pets.

Different dogs

DOGS COME IN ALL SHAPES and sizes—there are over 190 types, or breeds, known around the world! Each breed is different, and needs different amounts of exercise, space, food, grooming, and love. So before you choose a puppy, learn about the breeds you are interested in, to help you choose the dog that suits your family best.

Yorkshire terriers are a breed of toy dog.

Dog breeds

Dogs that look alike come from the same breed and are called purebreds. They usually have predictable needs and personalities. Breeds are divided into seven main groups. They are shown here.

Learning about breeds will help you choose the right puppy for you.

Toy dogs

This Shih Tzu is one of the tiny breeds of dog known as toy dogs. They are full of personality and may bark a lot! Toy dogs don't need lots of walking.

Shih Tzu

Beagle

Hounds

Hounds were bred to be hunters and have a built-in desire to chase things. They can be harder to train than other breeds and are not ideal pets for first-time owners.

West Highland white terrier

Terriers

Breeds in the terrier group are tough and have strong personalities. They can be very lively and even aggressive. Most terriers are small or medium-sized.

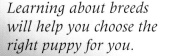

Rough collie

Sporting dogs

This group includes the Labrador retriever, the golden retriever, and most spaniels. Many breeds in this group are relaxed and easy to train. They are good with children and are popular family pets.

Cocker spaniel

Herding dogs

This group contains the collies and cattle dogs. They are intelligent breeds with lots of energy. This makes them easy to train. Herding dogs need lots to do, or they will get bored.

German shepherd

Non-sporting dogs

This contains all those breeds that don't fit into any other group! The poodle is part of this varied group.

Poodle

Working dogs

Working dogs often make better guard dogs than family pets, since they can be protective. The German shepherd is a well-known breed in this group.

Mixed-breed dogs

Some dogs are a mix of two or more breeds. Many mixed-breed dogs make loving, happy pets. They are usually healthier than purebreds. It is harder to predict how they will grow up or how easy they will be to train.

Mixed-breed dogs come in all shapes and sizes!

Early life

Puppies learn as they play together.

WHEN A PUPPY IS BORN, her eyes are closed and she can't hear. She's helpless. For the first few weeks of her life, her mother gives her all the milk, love, and care she needs. By the age of six weeks or so, a puppy will be much more independent. Most puppies are ready to leave their mothers and go to new homes when they are seven or nine weeks old.

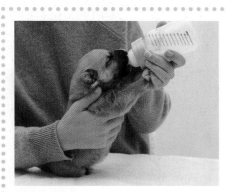

HELPING HAND

Sometimes a mother dog has so many puppies that she can't give them all enough milk. If this happens, some puppies need to be bottle-fed. The owner helps the mother dog by giving the smaller puppies a special milk substitute from a baby bottle.

Growing up

Puppies grow up much more quickly than human babies. At four weeks, they can run around and play. At five weeks, they have their first teeth! By about six months, they are almost full-grown.

Puppies snuggle up to each other for warmth.

HOW A PUPPY GROWS FROM ONE TO NINE WEEKS

One week old

The new puppy sleeps most of the time. She drinks milk from her mother if she is hungry.

Two weeks old

The puppy opens her eyes. It takes another week for her to see and hear properly.

Three weeks old

The puppy starts to explore the world around her. She still needs plenty of sleep.

Mother licks her puppies to keep them clean.

Puppy drinks milk from its mother.

This mother will stay close to her puppies for about two weeks.

Four weeks old

Puppies start to play together. She is growing quickly and becoming more independent.

Five weeks old

The puppy has all her milk teeth. She is eating solid food instead of drinking milk.

Nine weeks old

The puppy is old enough for you to pick her up and bring her home.

Finding a puppy

THERE ARE LOTS OF WAYS to find a new puppy. If you would like a purebred dog, ask the local veterinarian for help, and contact the breed club for a list of recommended breeders with puppies for sale. The vet may also know of mixed-breed puppies looking for a home. You can also call a local animal shelter or rescue group. They often need to find homes for unwanted puppies.

Purebred pups, such as these Australian sheep dogs, cost a lot more than mixed-breed puppies.

Purebred puppies

You can usually visit a breeder to look at a litter of puppies when the litter is about four weeks old. (You can't take the puppy you choose home until he is around nine weeks old.) Watch the mother of the puppies and see if she behaves in a nice way. Her puppies may grow up to be just like her.

Watch your puppy with her brothers and sisters to see how she behaves around other dogs.

Try to get to know a puppy before you decide to take him home.

Mixed breeds

If you would like to own a mixed-breed puppy, try to meet one of his parents too, for an idea of how big he will grow. If you can't do this, look at the puppy's paws. If he has big paws, he will probably grow into a big dog.

PUPPY MILLS

Avoid buying a puppy from a puppy mill. These are places where large numbers of puppies are bred purely for profit. The puppies can be unhealthy, and may have behavioral problems.

A healthy puppy

You can tell a lot about your puppy's personality and health at your first meeting. She should be lively and friendly, with a clean coat, even under her tail near her bottom. Remember to ask your vet to check your puppy's health, once you bring the pup home.

Your puppy should have bright eyes.

1 Check your puppy's nose is cool and damp when you touch it and, like the eyes, has no runny discharge.

2 Check her ears for black ear wax, which is a sign of mites. Mites can be treated easily. Ask your vet's advice.

3 Check her coat for evidence of fleas. Like ear mites, they are easily treated, using the correct products.

4 Check your puppy's feet. She should have five toes on the front paws, and four toes on the back paws.

Pet stores sell safe puppy toys, which your puppy can't swallow whole or chew apart. Don't give your puppy your own old toys.

Getting ready

IT'S A BIG CHANGE for your puppy when he leaves his mother. You can help him settle in to his new home by getting everything ready before he arrives. Buy the things you will need to care for him, and make sure your home is a safe place for a puppy to play. Puppies don't like lots of change all at once, so if you can buy the food that he is used to eating, he will be happier.

Safety

When your puppy explores your home, he might want to chew things. Take a look around each room first and put things that could hurt him out of his reach. Keep poisonous cleaning fluids in a cupboard with a safety latch. Don't leave knives, scissors, or small objects like buttons lying around.

SAFETY TIPS

- Unplug electrical goods so your puppy won't get a deadly shock if he tries to chew the cords.
- Put garbage in puppy-proof cans.
- Don't let your puppy eat houseplants. They might make him sick.
- Fence in or cover swimming pools or ponds.
- If your yard has a fence, keep the gate closed.

Busy times

Sometimes you will need to do things without your puppy getting in your way. While you are busy, keep him in a crate or behind a baby gate so he can't get into trouble. Choose a quiet place to put the crate, where your puppy can see you. Give him toys, water to drink, and a blanket to sit on. Put some newspaper in the crate in case he has an accident.

A baby gate is a good tool for keeping puppies out of trouble.

What to buy

You should buy your puppy a bed, puppy food, a bowl for food, a different bowl for water, toys, a collar with an name tag, and a leash. You will also need cleaning liquids and old newspapers to use until your puppy is housebroken.

YOU WILL NEED

Separate water and food bowls

Puppy food

Toys and chews

Nylon or leather collar, with identity tag

A leash for walks

Old newspaper

Cleaning materials

Line your puppy's bed with a cozy blanket.

A puppy chew will help your puppy's teeth.

Coming home

YOU'LL BE VERY EXCITED when it's time to pick up your new pet. It's a big day for you, but it's an even bigger one for your puppy. He will be leaving his mother, brothers and sisters, and everything he knows, and he might get upset or worried on the trip home. If this happens, you can help him if you keep calm and quiet. Talk to your puppy in a gentle voice, and let him know that everything will be fine.

Confident puppies generally accept change very easily.

Traveling

Bring your puppy home in a large cardboard box or a puppy crate, lined with newspaper and a blanket. If it is the first time that your puppy has been in a car, he might get carsick. Don't worry about this. Regular, short trips should get him used to car travel.

Pet carrier with air holes in the sides

You can buy pet carriers at most pet stores.

Introduce your puppy to his new home slowly. Let him look around from his pet carrier first.

Arriving home

Some puppies are put in puppy pens when they first get to their new homes. This is because they feel safer in small places. They eat and sleep there, and can be shut in if you need to go out. You shouldn't leave a puppy alone for the first few days. After that, he should only be left for a few hours at any time.

Keep a bowl of fresh drinking water in your puppy's pen.

Bathroom break

As soon as you get home, put your puppy in the yard or on newspaper to relieve himself. Look happy and say "good job" if he does the right thing. There are bound to be a few accidents at first.

Other pets

Other pets in your home might be jealous of the new puppy. Introduce them to your new dog carefully. Watch over their first few meetings and make sure your pets play nicely and don't fight.

Feeding

TO STAY HEALTHY, your puppy needs to eat the right amount of the right food, at regular times. Give her special puppy food and not adult dog food. Your vet, or the breeder, can give you a diet sheet that shows what she should eat, depending on her age. Make any changes to her diet bit by bit, so she has time to get used to them.

Small puppies have small stomachs, so they eat little and often.

What to feed

There are three main kinds of puppy food. A "complete" food contains everything a puppy needs, so you won't have to add anything. It can be canned or dry and is easy to store. Or you might want to feed your puppy canned or fresh meat. You should mix these foods with puppy kibble, to give her a balanced diet.

Complete canned food

Complete dry food

Chicken meat with puppy kibble

1 Be careful with hygiene when you prepare your puppy's meal. Put her food bowl on a paper towel so it doesn't touch the kitchen countertops.

2 Your puppy should not be possessive about her food or rush to eat it. To stop this from happening, offer her a tidbit before letting her eat.

HOW MANY MEALS?

Age	Meals per day
8–12 weeks	4 meals
13–16 weeks	3 meals
6 months	2 meals
10 months	2 meals (small breeds); 1 main meal and one smaller one (large breeds)

Cleaning up

After your puppy is done eating, wash her food bowl. This is a good time to wash and refill her water bowl, too.

After feeding a tidbit to your puppy, wash your hands.

RULES OF FEEDING

1. Set regular meal times.

2. Make sure your puppy always has a bowl of fresh water to drink.

3. Give your pet puppy food, not dog food. Puppies need different diets than adult dogs.

4. Weigh your puppy every week to find out how much food you need to feed her.

5. Don't make sudden changes to a puppy's diet. Do it slowly.

6. Don't give your dog too much to eat. Fat dogs do not live as long as trim, sleek dogs.

7. The ASPCA doesn't advise giving human food to pets.

8. Give your puppy proper dog treats as a reward for doing the right thing—but not too often!

9. Never give your puppy chocolate.

3 You should then be welcome when your dog eats, since she will see you as the person who gives her food. Never approach your puppy from behind while she is eating—this may startle her.

Take your pet to the vet in a pet carrier.

Meet the vet

YOU SHOULD TAKE YOUR PUPPY to the veterinarian the day after you bring him home. The vet will check the puppy and give your pet the shots he needs to stay well. It's a good idea find a vet close to your home, so you can get there quickly in an emergency.

First appointment

Try to see the vet at either the beginning or the end of clinic hours. This way, your puppy won't meet other animals until he has been fully vaccinated.

1 The vet will look your puppy over carefully to make sure he is healthy. He will look at his eyes, ears, teeth, jaws, and coat, and feel his tummy for any swellings that shouldn't be there.

2 Your puppy might have long nails, since he hasn't had any walks to wear them down yet. If so, the vet will trim them.

Reassure your puppy if he is worried by his first visit to the vet.

3 The vet will listen to your puppy's heart through a stethoscope, which makes his heartbeat easier to hear.

Protecting your puppy

Your vet will give your puppy injections to protect him from dangerous illnesses. The puppy usually has his first injection when he is 6 or 8 weeks old, but he will need to come back later for more shots. The vet will tell you when to bring the puppy back.

RABIES

Most communities require all dogs to have injections to protect them against a serious illness called rabies. Your vet will know about this.

It is important to protect your puppy from disease.

Healthcare

YOUR VET knows a lot about puppies. He can tell you how to protect your puppy's health. He can answer any questions you might have, too. You will have to do some things every day, or every week, to care for your puppy. The vet can explain why these things matter, and show you and your parents exactly how to do them.

When you hold your pet keep one arm under his bottom.

Identity chips are as small as a grain of rice.

Identity chips

In some places, your vet can help you keep your pet safe by injecting a tiny microchip into his neck. If your puppy gets lost, the chip can be scanned by the police. It tells people how to find you so they can return the puppy to you.

Worming

You must "worm" your puppy every three months to get rid of tiny worms in his tummy. The vet will give you the correct dosage based on your puppy's weight. Usually you'll mix a powder or pill into your pet's next meal.

Worming tablet being given with dried food

Small toothbrush

Tooth and nail

Clean your puppy's teeth every day with a dog toothbrush and animal toothpaste. Your vet can show you what to do. Clipping nails has to be done very carefully, because your puppy's nails will bleed if they are cut too short. Leave this job to your parents.

Finger toothbrush

Clippers

Clean the outside of your puppy's teeth

Every day
- Feed your puppy.
- Fill up his water bowl.
- Brush his teeth.
- Practice training.
- Spend time grooming your puppy. Make sure his eyes and ears are clean and his paws are not sore.

Every week
- Weigh your puppy to check he is getting the right amount of food for his size.
- Make sure his collar fits.

Other times
- Worm every three months
- Annual booster injections

Keeping records

Keep all your puppy's records in a file or folder. Store his vaccination certificate, photographs, and other papers inside. You should also write down when his next booster injections and worming tablets are due.

Vaccination certificate

File holding puppy's records

Poodle puppy

Soft puppy toy being used as a comforter

Puppies learn quickly, so try to follow a routine from the start.

Settling in

IT IS A GOOD IDEA TO teach your puppy your family's rules from the very beginning. She will need to know where she goes to the bathroom, and where she eats and sleeps. She also needs to learn how to be alone. Your puppy might be upset at night when you and your family go to bed. If she starts to whine, don't go to her. She will fall asleep in the end. In a few days, she will get used to sleeping by herself.

Bedtime

Play with your puppy for a while before you go to bed. This will tire her out so she feels like sleeping. At night, leave the radio on so your puppy can hear voices and doesn't feel lonely. Put a warm hot-water bottle wrapped in a blanket in her crate, so she can snuggle against it.

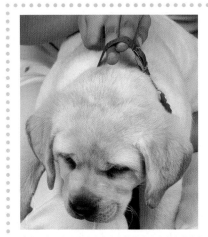

FITTING A COLLAR

You should get your puppy used to her collar as soon as possible. Make sure it fits properly. You should be able to get two fingers between the collar and your puppy's neck. She may scratch the collar at first, but will soon forget about it—especially if you distract her with a game!

Puppies often sniff around before and after going to the bathroom, too.

Housebreaking

Teach your puppy where he is allowed to go to the bathroom. Pick a place outside, and take him there every two hours. He will need to go after food or a nap. Take him to the same place every time. Wait until he goes, even if it takes a few minutes. Then pet and praise him when he does the right thing.

Which name?

Choose a short name for your puppy, like Daisy or Rusty. Avoid names such as Bo or Kit, which sound like command words. Use her name as often as you can. She will quickly get used to it and come when you call her.

1 To teach your puppy her name, sit or kneel on the floor with your arms out and call to her in a friendly voice.

2 If your puppy comes to you, show her you are pleased. Give her a treat. (Later, you can replace treats with hugs).

3 By getting down with your puppy, you help her learn not to jump up. She is then less likely to do it as she gets bigger.

When your puppy knows her name, you can start to train her.

Grooming

Dogs with long fur need lots of grooming.

GROOM YOUR PUPPY every day. This will keep her coat soft, clean, and free of tangles. It is also a good time to make sure there are no fleas or ticks in her fur, or mites or grass seeds in her ears. Finally, it helps you to teach your puppy that she must sit still sometimes, even if she wants to move around. This is an important lesson for a puppy.

Brush or comb?

There are lots of different grooming tools. Ask the breeder or the vet which type is best for your puppy's fur. Some dogs have unusual fur, such as poodles with their curly coats. They may need to visit a grooming salon to keep their coats looking good.

Poodle fur needs special grooming care.

Comb

Pad

Brush

Daily brushing

If you brush your pet every day, you take away most of her loose hairs and help keep your home neat! Otherwise dogs can shed a lot of hair around your home, especially in the spring, when they lose their thick winter fur.

Long, silky coats take time to comb.

BATHING

Try not to bathe a puppy under 6 months old. If she is really dirty, rinse her with plain water. Dry mud will usually just brush out.

1 Get your puppy used to being groomed a little at a time. Pet her until she settles down and then start to brush her gently. Always begin on the body.

2 Gradually move down her front and back legs to her feet. If the hair between her toes needs trimming, cut it carefully. Remember to use round-ended scissors.

3 Next, brush her head and ears. The skin inside her ears is very delicate, so brush and comb them gently. Finally, clean her eyes using a pet tissue.

Never use human shampoo on a puppy.

Wipe down and away from the eye when cleaning it.

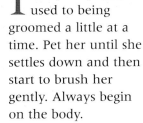

4 Your puppy may sleep after she has been groomed. This is because she is happy and feels totally relaxed.

Dog talk

Is your puppy panting? Then he feels hot!

THERE ARE LOTS OF WAYS that your puppy can tell you how he is feeling. He might bark when he wants something, or wag his tail when he's happy. If you learn to understand what your puppy is saying, it will help you when you start to train him.

Barking

Puppies bark when they are excited. They also bark to get your attention when they want to play or go to the bathroom. Older puppies bark if someone comes to the door or if they hear a strange sound. This is a warning bark. It's easy to tell the two barks apart.

Puppies hold their heads high when they bark.

A wagging tail

Your puppy's tail shows you how he is feeling. He wags his tail from side to side when he's happy or excited. If his tail is standing straight up, he's being very alert and aware. And when your puppy is sad, he'll curl his tail between his legs.

Spend lots of time with your puppy, so that you learn to love and trust each other.

Making a fuss over your dog is nice for both of you!

CHEWING

Does your puppy chew a lot? If she is under seven months, she is probably teething. If she chews things after that, she is doing it to learn about her surroundings. Give her lots of dog chews to bite on, so she won't chew the furniture!

Guard dogs

As puppies grow older, they start to protect their homes. They bark to warn you when a stranger comes to the door.

German shepherds make good guard dogs, but must be properly trained.

29

Know your puppy

WILD DOGS LIVE IN FAMILY groups called packs. One dog is the leader. He makes sure the others follow the rules. All the dogs have a place in the pack, but some dogs are more dominant (have more power) than others. When you get a dog, you and your family become his "pack." If he knows that your parents lead the pack, and understands his place, he will be happy to follow your rules.

When a puppy rolls over to have his tummy rubbed, he's also showing that he knows you are the boss!

Body language

A puppy uses his whole body to express himself. He will be bouncy when he's playing and sad if you scold him. He may spring to attention, for example, if he sees or hears another dog. The hairs, or "hackles", along the middle of his his back may stand up. His ears, tail, and hair show his mood.

In a pack of foxhounds, some dogs have higher status than other dogs.

The dominant puppy stands while the other rolls over.

Curled tail

Play-bow

If your puppy wants you to play with him, he will crouch down with his bottom in the air. This is called a play-bow. Then he'll wag his tail and bark to get your attention.

The senses

A puppy hears and smells things better than a human can. She will know when there is someone at the door before the doorbell rings, and will prick up her ears to see if she knows who the visitor is.

Ears beginning to prick up

Alert

An alert puppy will listen and sniff the air. If she needs to investigate further, she will leap up for a closer look. She can spot movement more quickly than a human can, but she doesn't see color in the same way.

Submissive body language

This puppy's pricked ears and fixed stare show she is alert.

Sad

If your puppy is naughty and you scold her, she will look sad, putting her ears down and her tail between her legs. She may crouch down or roll over on her back to say "sorry."

31

Making friends

ONE OF THE BEST things you can do for your puppy is teach her about the world around her. The most important time to do this is when she is between eight and twelve weeks old. Introduce her to as many people, sights, and sounds as you can. Then she will find it easier to take everything in stride as she gets older and goes out for walks.

The first person a puppy bonds with is her new owner.

Meeting the family

Your puppy may be easily scared at first, so introduce other family members and pets carefully. Ask everyone to sit on the floor. If your puppy goes up to them, they can make a fuss over her. Otherwise, they should leave her alone to explore in her own time.

Puppies and kittens can become good friends.

CHECKLIST

- Never rush your puppy.
- Watch over your puppy when she meets other pets.
- Introduce your puppy to as many different people and situations as possible.

Puppy kindergarten

Ask your vet if there is a puppy kindergarten in your area. This is a good place for you to introduce your puppy to other pets, so you can teach her how to behave with other dogs as well as people.

A puppy can go to "kindergarten" from the age of 12 weeks.

Your puppy should meet lots of different people.

Meeting people

Don't wait for a party to start introducing your puppy to new people. Ask your friends over to play, or carry your puppy to the park or down your street so she can meet your neighbors.

If your puppy is friendly, you can take her with you to all kinds of places!

Your puppy will meet strange dogs on her walks. These meetings should be friendly.

A friendly puppy

The more things your puppy does while she is young, the better. However, always make sure that she's enjoying herself. If she backs away from something, you may be rushing her. Slow down, and give your puppy more time. Don't fuss over her—she will discover things when she's ready.

Your puppy may not want to walk on a leash at first!

How to train

IT'S UP TO YOU and your family to teach your puppy how to behave. Show your puppy what you want him to do, and reward him at once when he gets it right! Start training him right away, even just for a few minutes a day. It should be fun for you both, but remember, you are teaching your puppy, not playing a game. Be patient and don't give up!

Starting out

As well as housebreaking, teach your puppy his name first of all (see p.25). He also needs to understand the word "no," so that you can stop him from getting into trouble. Always say "no" in a firm voice. Don't laugh, even if your puppy is doing something funny. Your puppy cannot understand human language, so try to make your body signals match your words.

Boy waves finger to back up saying "no"

PATIENCE

Always be patient with your puppy. Make sure the whole family uses the same words, such as "OK," when training her. Don't lose your temper when things go wrong. Never, ever hit your puppy.

Rewards

When your puppy does the right thing, praise or hug him right away. He'll see that doing what you ask brings rewards! End training sessions on a good note, with something your puppy can do well.

Let your puppy play with his favorite toy after a good training session, to reward him.

Discipline

Sometimes you will have to punish your puppy for being naughty, or for biting hard when you are playing. Ignore your puppy and don't look at him. He'll know he has done something wrong and will quickly learn to stop it.

Be consistent with your puppy— this helps him to learn.

WAITING

Your puppy should stand or sit quietly while you prepare his food. He should also wait until you have put his dish down and moved away before he starts to eat. Follow this house rule from day one. Often, all you need to do is ask your puppy to "wait" while you're putting out his food, then tell him "OK" in a firm voice.

Training

THE BEST AGE FOR TRAINING your puppy is between the ages of three and six months. He will soon learn to do what you ask if you praise and reward him when he's good and show that you're disappointed with him if he's naughty. You can teach him to sit, lie down, and do other tricks. He also needs to learn how to behave on the leash when you go out for walks. If you want to do more with your puppy, find out if your local dog club runs an obedience class that you can go to.

Puppies are fast learners and eager to please.

Sitting

Teach your puppy to sit. Call his name to get his attention. When he is standing in front of you, show him a treat. Move it slowly back over his head. Your puppy will have to sit down so that he can keep watching the treat.

At this point, say "sit" in a firm voice. When he sits down, show him you're pleased by giving him the treat and praising him.

Eventually your puppy will learn to do the right thing.

Your puppy might jump up for the treat instead of sitting! Keep calm and try again.

TRAINING TIP

Always say your puppy's name first to get his attention. Then give a command, such as "sit," in a firm but friendly voice.

Lying down

Ask your puppy to sit. Hold a treat under her nose, then move it down to the floor. Your puppy will follow the food with her nose. Move the treat forward. As your puppy stretches out to reach it, say "down." Give her the treat and praise her when she's down.

Fetch

Puppies love to chase and fetch toys. Throw a toy for your puppy. As she runs after it, say her name and "fetch" in a friendly voice. As she brings it back to you, hold out your hand, say her name, and ask her to "bring" the toy to you.

1 This puppy is learning to fetch toys but has yet to learn to bring them back.

2 Never chase your puppy if she refuses to give you a toy. You will be giving her the wrong signal. Instead of teaching her to fetch, she'll think you're playing chase.

DOG CLUBS

Before joining a dog club, go to a meeting as a visitor, without your puppy, to get an idea of what is involved.

First walks

IT'S AN EXCITING DAY when you take your puppy for his first walk. Remember, there are dangers for a puppy outside, and it's up to you to keep him safe and under control. Don't let your puppy run off, especially near a road, and bear in mind that other people might not like dogs as much as you do.

Fasten the leash to your puppy before you go out so he can't run away.

Walking on a leash

Taking your puppy for walks is fun as long as she behaves. If your puppy starts to pull, stand still. When she looks back to see why you stopped, ask her to "come." Praise her for doing so, and walk backward a few steps before continuing forward. She will soon learn that she will reach the park sooner if she walks by your side instead of rushing ahead of you.

Walk to an open space where your puppy has plenty of room to play.

1 It's important to train your puppy to cross the street safely. Keep the leash short so she can't run ahead of you.

2 Your puppy must learn to sit and wait until the road is clear. Make sure she knows it's wrong to chase cyclists or cars.

3 When it is safe to cross, tell your puppy to walk on by your side. She should do this quietly and not rush forward.

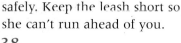

Drying off

If your puppy gets wet during a walk, rub him dry so that he doesn't get cold. Be gentle with his paws.

SCOOPING UP

Take a plastic bag or pooper scooper along so you can clean up after your puppy if he goes to the bathroom while you're out.

!

Children walking with a puppy should always be accompanied by a responsible adult.

Playing

PUPPIES LOVE TO PLAY. Playing teaches them about the world around them and helps to keep them fit and happy. Even young puppies enjoy games of fetch. Older puppies enjoy playing hide-and-seek with hidden toys, which they find using their great sense of smell.

A ball is a good toy for a puppy. Make sure it is big enough that your puppy can't swallow it.

Which toy?

There are lots of toys that you can buy for puppies. They love soft toys, strong rubber toys that they can chew and chew, or toys that make a squeaky noise. Whichever toys you choose for your dog, don't let her be possessive about them. Never give your puppy your old toys—they may not be safe for her to chew.

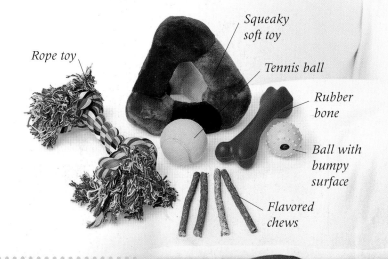

Rope toy

Squeaky soft toy

Tennis ball

Rubber bone

Ball with bumpy surface

Flavored chews

PLAY-BITING

Puppies play-bite their brothers and sisters. Teach your puppy not to bite you by stopping any game at once if she gets too excited or rough. She will soon learn to play more gently.

Tug-of-war

Your puppy will like playing tug-of-war, but it isn't a good game for her to learn. As puppies grow up, they can get very strong. When she's a grown dog, she might pull you over in a game, which will be no fun at all.

Playtime

Puppies enjoy all kinds of games. They will chase after balls, retrieve soft toys, and search for hidden toys. If you give your puppy a new toy, he'll probably get very excited. However, he should always give it back to you if you ask him for it.

Rope toys are fun to chew and are good for games of fetch, too.

1 This puppy has a new toy. He wags his tail and pounces on it in excitement. He then finds out the new toy squeaks.

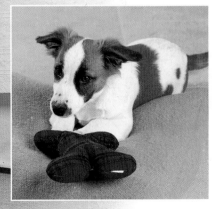

2 Next, he mouths and rolls on the toy. This marks it with his scent. He may also carry the toy around with him for awhile.

3 However much he likes his toy, he must give it up when you ask. Praise him so he knows he has done the right thing.

41

Illness

When a puppy feels unwell, he often looks sad. His nose may feel dry and warm instead of cool and wet.

AS YOU GET TO KNOW your puppy, you will see immediately when she is feeling ill. Until then, be careful, since young puppies can get sick very quickly. Luckily, they usually get better just as fast, and are soon back to normal and ready to play! If you think your puppy is seriously ill, take her to the vet immediately.

Look for symptoms

A sick puppy looks sad, won't play, and sleeps more than usual. If your puppy won't eat, make sure she's drinking—puppies get dehydrated quickly. If she's stretching a lot more than usual, she may have a tummy problem. If she is sick more than once, has diarrhea, or is not going to the bathroom as usual, it is also a cause for concern. Call the vet if you're worried.

CAR TRIPS

In warm weather, a dog left in a parked car can quickly get heatstroke, which is a life-threatening condition. If you must briefly leave your puppy in the car, park in the shade, leave a window open, make sure she has plenty of water to drink, and hurry back—*never* leave her for more than a few minutes.

Ear and eye drops

One day you or your parents may need to give your puppy ear or eye drops. Be calm and quiet when you do this, to help keep your puppy relaxed. Speak reassuringly and give your puppy a hug afterward.

Keep your puppy quiet and relaxed while you give him ear drops.

This puppy has an itch, but excessive scratching may be due to fleas.

Fleas

If your puppy is scratching more than usual, use a flea comb to check her for fleas. If you find fleas, treat your puppy promptly to avoid complications.

INSECT STINGS

If an insect bites or stings your puppy, it may cause a swelling. Sometimes these lumps appear on your puppy's face. A swelling on her nose or on her throat may make it hard for your puppy to breathe. To be safe, take her to the veterinarian at once to rule out a snake bite or an allergic reaction. The vet may give your puppy an injection to bring down the swelling.

Keep your sick puppy warm and comfortable as you travel to the veterinarian.

Emergencies

If your puppy is in pain, or bleeding from an injury, take her to the vet right away. She may have a serious problem, and a delay could be fatal. The pain may make your puppy crabby, so be gentle when taking her to the vet. Try to carry her in a crate, or a large box lined with a blanket, to avoid moving her around too much.

Puppy wrapped in a blanket to go to the vet

Growing up

YOUR PUPPY WILL GROW QUICKLY over her first year. In 'dog years', she is actually growing up about seven times faster than you are. Dogs can live for over 12 (human) years. Looking after an adult dog carries responsibilities for all your family to think about.

Most puppies reach full size by 6 months of age.

Neutering

During your first few months of puppy ownership, you will need to decide whether or not to have your puppy neutered. This operation will prevent your pet from having puppies of its own when it grows up. Female puppies mature at 6 to 8 months, male puppies at 8 to 12 months. Your vet can tell you about the operation and when it is best to carry it out.

Remember, if your female dog has puppies, you will have to find homes for all of them.

A change of diet

When your pet is full-grown, she will need to switch from puppy food to adult dog food. This change should be made slowly, over a few days, to avoid tummy upsets. As your dog ages, you may have to change her diet again. Ask your vet's advice about this.

Do not overfeed your dog. Fat dogs are unhealthy.

As your puppy grows, check the fit of her collar and loosen it as necessary. She may need a new collar sometimes.

Puppies grow quickly. At seven weeks (see p.25), this puppy barely reached the girl's knees. Now nine months old, she can easily reach her waist.

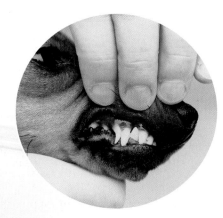

Dental care

Some puppies do not lose all their first teeth as they should. You may see the old teeth along with the new ones when you clean your puppy's teeth. Your vet can also check for them during a routine veterinary examination. First teeth that don't fall out on their own should be removed to prevent overcrowding.

GETTING OLDER

Older dogs do not walk as far as they once did because, like humans, they get stiff joints. They may also get a little deaf, something you should think about if they are off the leash. Older dogs may need a coat to keep them warm on cool days.

Popular dog data

THE TABLE BELOW shows the adult size of some of the more popular dog breeds. It also gives an idea of the amount of grooming and exercise each breed of dog needs. For further information, you can look at various web sites (see below).

Welsh terriers are medium-sized dogs.

Recommended web sites:
www.akc.org
www.hsus.org/ace/12561

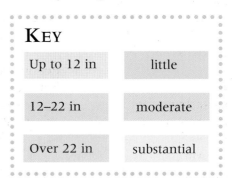

KEY

Up to 12 in	little
12–22 in	moderate
Over 22 in	substantial

BREED	SIZE	AMOUNT OF EXERCISE	AMOUNT OF GROOMING
Chihuahua (short coat)			
Chihuahua (long coat)			
Yorkshire terrier			
Australian silky terrier			
Maltese terrier			
Shih Tzu			
Dachshund (smooth coat)			
Dachshund (long coat)			
Dachshund (wire coat)			
Toy poodle			
West Highland white			
Cavalier King Charles			
Poodle (Mini/Standard)			
Cocker spaniel			
Australian cattle dog			
English springer spaniel			
Beagle			
Staffordshire bull terrier			
Border collie			
Labrador retriever			
Golden retriever			
German shepherd			
Boxer			
Rough collie			
Doberman pinscher			

The silhouettes show the average height of a ten-year-old child and the adult height of a small, medium, and large dog.

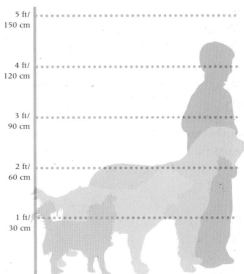

5 ft/ 150 cm

4 ft/ 120 cm

3 ft/ 90 cm

2 ft/ 60 cm

1 ft/ 30 cm

Index

ACKNOWLEDGMENTS

DORLING KINDERSLEY WOULD LIKE TO THANK:

The Mayhew Animal Home for Benjy the mixed-breed puppy;

the Richbourne Kennels for Star, Buttons, and Fliss the Labrador retrievers;

Suzanne and Molly, her Hungarian vizsla;

Hope and Ruby, her wirehaired fox terrier;

Milo and Snoop, his Welsh terrier;

Tony and Rocco, his Jack Russell cross.

MODELS

Amber, Jasmine, Benetta, Milo, Charlie, and Joe